COLOSSEUM

Books by Katie Ford

Deposition
Storm (chapbook)
Colosseum

COLOSSEUM

Poems by
Katie Ford

Graywolf Press

Publication of this volume is made possible in part by a grant provided by the Minnesota State Arts Board, through an appropriation by the Minnesota State Legislature; a grant from the Wells Fargo Foundation Minnesota; and a grant from the National Endowment for the Arts, which believes that a great nation deserves great art. Significant support has also been provided by the Bush Foundation; Target; the McKnight Foundation; and other generous contributions from foundations, corporations, and individuals. To these organizations and individuals we offer our heartfelt thanks.

Published by Graywolf Press
250 Third Avenue North, Suite 600
Minneapolis, Minnesota 55401
All rights reserved.

www.graywolfpress.org

Published in the United States of America

ISBN 978-1-55597-501-2

2 4 6 8 9 7 5 3

Library of Congress Control Number: 2007940215
Cover design: Christa Schoenbrodt, Studio Haus
Cover photograph: Katie Ford

Acknowledgments

My gratitude to the editors of the following journals and presses who first printed these poems:

Alaska Quarterly: "Earth, This Firelit Lantern"

American Literary Review: "Flee," "Tell Us," "Crossing America," "He Said," "Fish Market," "Tess," "Rose," "Snow," "Tolstoy's Storm," "Divining Stick"

American Poetry Review: "Colosseum," "Koi," "Duomo," "What We Get," "The Shape of Us," "Overture," "Beirut," "Earth [Who sees our gestures . . .]," "Rarely," "Earth [If you respect . . .]," "Coliseum Theater"

Barrow Street: "Easter Evening"

Caffeine Destiny: "Ark," "Spring Wish," "The Singing"

Cairn: "Cemetery"

Canteen: "The Vessel Bends the Water"

Harvard Divinity Bulletin: "Flag," "Snakes"

Intersection/New Orleans (Press Street): "Rose"

Paris Review: "Earth [Wild horses folded . . .]"

Phoebe: "Injury"

Pleiades: "Raised Voice"

Poetry International: "Vessel"

Seneca Review: "Division"

Underwood: A Broadside Anthology (Underwood Press): "Earth [Who sees our gestures . . .]"

"Colosseum" was anthologized in *Legitimate Dangers: Poets of a New Century* (Sarabande Books, 2006).

Marick Press printed "Storm" as a chapbook in 2007. My thanks to Ilya Kaminsky and Mariela Griffor.

Many thanks to the PEN American Center and to Loyola University New Orleans for grants toward the completion of this volume.

I especially would like to thank the writers who were such generous critics of this book during its composition: Tess Gallagher, Josh Emmons, Mary Szybist, Ilya Kaminsky, Susan Lynch, and Shane McCrae.

for Josh
&
for Tess

Contents

III. Colosseum

there, as here, ruin opens
the tomb, the temple; enter

H.D.

BEIRUT

Ruin is a promise
we make to each other:
I am born the day Saigon falls
and Lebanon takes to its own throat a club.

On that day
southern soldiers tear their uniforms
for the Saigon River to bear
to open water. The lucky are in boats,
their papers burnt into red locusts of no detail,
a swarm of no birth, no party, in flight, in fall
back toward the river of garments
drenched of each frantic gesture
that pointed to the cryptic sea.

For two days my mother lies flat with pain.
The locusts have traveled far into her radio,
their bodies cast with boat-shaped tips
while not even our fingers stay together
to scull us from cities where salt water, years later,
will pour up the neck of each great live oak.

By transistor she hears the fall of Saigon
and Lebanon's night-coins of bulleted light.

The radio needs almost nothing to pick up the world, she says.

She'll wake to it, she'll sleep to it,
she'll tell it what she wishes.

As a child I'll watch her turn
the small dome of the dial
in which many lives crowd
to transmit the yellowing conditions
of each country's eye.

Lebanon of limestone, Lebanon of sheep,
for two days my mother lies flat.
On the third day
the goats of the Lebanese hills
tilt their heads, stop their feed and hear
an ancient city begin to break itself in half—
and half again—
and once more—
until the halves are dust
in which the olives will not fatten.

Only echoes grow from the limestone
as screeching birds carry
what sounds are human
to the white cliff to cry them out.

A human cry lives many lives.
The gulls are that fierceness made flesh.

For thirty years the people of my life lived.
Then thousands around me drowned.

Saigon, Phuket, Beirut, your gulls
flew over America and lent her your name:

If it is as Socrates says,
that locusts were human
until they heard the song of the world
and, so captured, forgot
to eat and drink and died—

and if it's true the gods
took pity on the dead
enough to resurrect them
into ashen singing things—

then, so too, our songs

will have to be plagues.

I

Storm

He who slept on the roof died on the roof
He who slept in the house had no burial

LAMENT, 2100 B.C.

FLEE

When the transistor said *killing wind*
I felt myself a small noise

a call sign rubbed out
but still live where light
cut through the floorboards

and don't you think I dreamed the light a sign

didn't I want to cross
the water of green beads breaking
where one saw the other last

where the roof was torn
and the dome cried out
that the tearing was wide and far

and this is not just a lesson
of how to paint an X upon a house
how to mark one dead in the attic
two on the floor

didn't I wish
but didn't I flee

when the cries fell through
the surface of light
and the light stayed light
as if to say nothing or

what do you expect me to do

I am not human

I gave you each other
so save each other.

TELL US

the radio is coming in
all over us a caller asks what will

be done for the animals
of the zoo the oil rigs

at sea the stranded
of the dome

first the storm
will take all lanterns all flags

it will begin at 600 hours
end at 1300 at which time

your absolute nakedness
the barest accident of you

will stand before its organized eye
therefore ready yourself

but do not panic
you cannot be ready

RARELY

Rarely do I remember another month, August.
Rarely another day do I remember.

I threw tarps over a life
and never could they reach—

still hastily I gathered
tarps more rare by the hour

in the city of nothing to spare.
I draped true but thin shores

for the shipwreck
as the radio said:

Rarely does as rarely has
grown tired of not doing.

Take your rarities.
Take your household gods.

If you have no gods:
make them.

EARTH

If you respect the dead
and recall where they died
by this time tomorrow
there will be nowhere to walk.

ARK

We love the stories of flood and the few
told to prepare in advance by their god.
In that story, the saved are
always us, meaning:
whoever holds the book.

FISH MARKET

Now the suicidal drift
toward the market along the river.

Blue tarps drape the oysters
harvested from contaminated beds,
silverlings caught from trestles of the resealed lake,

their eyes against the also-open eyes
of hundreds in the sudden underneath.

What is there now to eat? Here:
fish unfold from their skins.
It is meat, you don't have
to look anymore. Disaster

eats what there is. It is
biblical: sit at the table of another
country, you must eat
what is set before you.

They didn't know they were in another country
until they were left living.

Confused by hunger,
they fill their bags.

VESSEL

We were hardly vessels
what we took in could not be

and so we spat it out as dogs spit out
the wretched fish the only meat

we were not mules
though we put stores on our backs

half-finished stories
thin mothers in frames

we were never vessels
but I wanted so much to be and swallow and

carry and bear and not have a mind to mind
nor a mouth to spit nor a heart

to tear into strips of weed
from the sea.

HE SAID

that city needed a good cleaning he said
my buddy he's in the guard he said

there were things going on down there
the public doesn't even know about

what killings I said of citizens I said
don't worry he said not innocent ones

you should have heard my buddy he said

TOLSTOY'S STORM

And I quit going hunting with a gun,
so that I would not be too easily tempted
to rid myself of life.

TOLSTOY

I dreamt the earth was dry
undrowned it could speak again

a red tree appeared as I walked
and for a moment

I no longer mourned
nor had to hide the rope from myself

as Tolstoy did all autumn inside me.

SNOW

I held the chambered gun
and clicked its emptiness against the crows

let them fly inside me even as they fell
back into the saplings of thin woods

for when there is no storm
there is this stormed body

to keep alive in its solitary room
outside of which the snow is falling

one of us at a time.

II

Vessel

I didn't want this, not
  this (but listen, quietly,
to want is what bodies do
  and now we are ghosts only).

MARINA TSVETAEVA

THE SHAPE OF US

Perhaps our difficult loneliness
was not given to us
but was ours by mistake
like an early theory of the world
in which all creation was a single sun,
in which humans and trees
and the white heron bent to feed
were not forms but caverns
cutting into that light. Pompeii was discovered
beneath calcifications of ash
because certain hollows looked human.

Likewise every so often five feet of Nagasaki
was less charred where the bodies
had absorbed all they could. A cold spot greened
the ocean that day, the stinging
fish descended like rows of bells
let slowly down from their ropes—let down, let go
as the mind drifts long, drifts
far from beliefs that cannot hold.

When I stood in the American city, bells
inside the walls wore on, not ringing
for us but for their own death,
that it might come now, and quickly.
Something please tell me I'm wrong
about impermanence,
wrong there is no unbroken believable thing
on this earth.

CROSSING AMERICA

Days you can't eat, days
food doesn't occur to you.

Then you are able, you eat what's before you
and again in your imagination
you eat. The pattern works like happiness

but the dog doesn't like it. He swims
his paws against the dry air of the Grand Canyon
as you hold him over the rail.

He will like the beaches of Santa Cruz,
where he will run past the dead tonnage
of seal lifted and abandoned
by the astonished law of water,

law that can pull the heavy dead back
or push them away,

but never by any human wish.

DIVISION

We drove through Wyoming passing people on horseback, noon horse shadows like those of caskets lifted up, the dead sitting up through pine boxes, looking at the strange reins in their hands. Once we were in the mountains we saw no animals, no birds. Green signs beside the granite rocks dated them back to the Triassic Age, Mississippian. On the opposing hill, the trail the goats wore down coming to water curved like a strand of hair, a single hair, unmassed. You said stop the car. Look at that, you said, pointing at the strips of ice-age rock, settling. A mountain range is simply a crease in the land is how it was taught to me. A crease is the foresight of division, you were taught. Desperate for communion, Catherine of Siena was beside herself in hills like these, eating nothing but an herb she would suck on and spit out. She scalded herself at the baths, ran away to a cave, shoved twigs into her mouth so that when the host traveled down her raw throat she would indeed feel something, even a god breaking inside her. Would you look at that, you said again near the rail of the viewpoint, where the historical marker explained the plates underneath. Beneath it, a crow's wing. Lord of confusion, Lord of great slaughter and thin birds, you could never answer all of us at once. Layer by layer I imagined pulling it apart to find the upholding musculature beneath the soot and grease of flight. Finding none—just the spinelike axis and its branching barbs, minute hooks holding them together—we continued on to the hotel parking lot in Sheridan, where at night someone scraped a key or a knife alongside the car while we slept off what we could. It was hard to tell what was used. There was nowhere to fix it. There was no talk of ever fixing it.

EARTH

Who sees what is between us? Who sees our gestures,
one frayed blue blanket thrown around the two of us,

and the things we do with our eyes, how we want
the ocean to eat everything dead.

I want something dragged across me as the gritty length
of sandbar suggests. You want nearly nothing, closing your eyes.

To have something obey us, something ignore us.
Who sees us plead? I can't stop looking at the two houses

lit off shore in which no one moves. I pick up shells,
but we are not like shells, there is no table to set us upon for judgment.

Why would there ever be such a place,
since we already believe

this blue blanket around us,
it is all that is around us, you and I—

INJURY

What we had were hooks
holding up the slim hospital curtain,
their cheap clanging
unlike any bell ringing out permanence,
the sound made more shallow
by the histories the sheet cornered off
but could not keep private.

I could see through it, the pleats of cotton—
I could see you, what was within me
was felled, the thought we could not be harmed.
I pushed it back, thin curtain—
when you saw me you said *you're here.*

THE VESSEL BENDS THE WATER

The body begs for a system that will not break—
even to fold the warm clothes, wanting
the edges to do as they are meant to do—
                                  this is why I touched him,
I could hardly touch him, I touched him for only
a short time and not for the reason he thought.
I had been thinking of the river before, its rocks bared
and dried and deeply summered.
But then reports came back of barges breaking
the levees, skiffs bent against boulders,
aluminum glistening from above
like the wet lid of some downturned eye
that is not ashamed but about to plead
for some just realized need,
an answer to all this death. But the earth sends
only Indian paintbrush—
the feathery plant that grows where an animal has died—
not as elegy but as substitute. Last night, things made
sudden by illness, I held
onto the kitchen counter, and this seems like nothing,
how I kept my hands there. Nothing, my hands on his stomach,
where small chinks had been taken out of his skin as if by a carver's tool.
And I know there is no retrieving it back: no retrieving any of it back:
the time the body, its tree-shadowed markings,
has been racked against the walls
with no one else, just highway,
just windows.
            Yet in those few times I touched him,
knowing one thing unfolded us both, it was my history beneath me,
my hands at least touching its skin.

TESS

To return I must triple myself with governmental tissue
someone misspelled my easy name upon

how will I be let back into the guarded city now
how is this no-one to go

I have been here before have fled things *Tess* I said
can I sleep in your library for the rest of my life

yes she said as she brought me a plate of salmon
from the Strait of Juan de Fuca

but in the library
there are many devastations

instead go back to your own—

THE SINGING

It was not sufficient to put wayward
bodies back into their tombs.

I walked through the flooded wards
but turned suddenly back:
there was only a sliver of land
where the dead had not drowned
and I was not on it.

I welded myself between the days
of January, February. But they sang
as I boiled parasites from the bath.
They sang as I lowered into that water.

I wanted a blue night with blue-white rings,
lifts of smoke-light from the centuried houses.
To be on the balcony with Josh,
with Martin and Rose, watching smoke from chimneys.

I wanted to see others alive
and count myself among them.

But they sang as I boiled parasites
from the bath. They sang
as I lowered into their water.

FLAG

Some come to this ruin and raise a flag.
Some take a prophet too soon by the hand.
The dead are still lost and the lost nearly dead:
Here a woman spills onto her porch to show
she has opened her wrists. What did she use?
She used the wind.

WHAT WE GET

I waited for a silence with its boards stripped off,
its sills pried away, all glasswork, all September light
with no latch. And when it came,

sometimes it was easy to think of nothing at all, have no question
at all, to sit and stare at the cracked, orange house next door
where the rodents scurried in and out, storing

green bulbs dropped from our trees—olive nuts, our choked-back eyes—
for the mild southern winter in which nothing dies,
only goes a way a while.

I wanted the far away. I wanted not to feel
caught. Look at the myrtle tree pulling up the yard.
Look at the belief I can't live by, how it didn't follow
but was here before me like the fields of tall, planted cane

where anything can be hidden. I think this is
what we get when we ask to be saved:
a land where everything grows, and there are many killings.

SPRING WISH

As from the Earth the light Balloon
Asks nothing but release—

EMILY DICKINSON

Some mornings there was bread on the air
and transoms opened to let the oaks wake you,
light chains of pollen caught on the dog's sleeping face.
And afternoons of parades, people dressed like ghosts
and cyclones, like government officials and a giraffe
on stilts, animal of the deep savannah we wished we stood on.
It is a far wish, a spring wish,
and so the people of the parade let go of
balloons they dreamt were their minds,
not the minds they woke to find writhing in the gravel,
but rising tangerine minds, porcelain white, blue
of a sky in which to be absolutely lost.
So much pleasure I remember
when mine slipped from sight
but could be imagined almost perfectly and gone,
warm on the string where I'd held it.

COLISEUM THEATER

for Josh

The houses burn, the oil rigs burn,
but when the oldest moviehouse burns,
our days are named by fires.
All the films we saw there, their reels melting, the rows
where lovers went because they knew
or didn't know, it doesn't matter,
that watching the same story
could make them closer.

Hearing the clicking of the same tapes,
the same rough frames clacking
like a priest's thurible, the smoky
black-and-whites drifting over the audience
watching the radiantly nimble actors
who loved and died
or loved and lived because something they wanted
to play *did* play, suddenly, on their phonograph.

All we had then was the movies.
Our own stories kept turning away—
we made silent, glassy agreements not to tell them.
But when the moviehouse burned, what were we
to say? We who wanted so much
to say again, simply,
let's go to the movies.
Please, just let us go.

CEMETERY

In its grasses the vault-filled cemetery swayed
with wind, yet dusked-down and tight, ruled.
The anticipatory lack inked onto whatever page
was left of us. We sat in the middle of it: trespass.
We laid down in the middle of it: falsity.
When you touched me,
I felt nothing. The day so beautiful
it struck me across the face.

RAISED VOICE

I had no craving. I heard sirens at night.
No craving, and a moon through the blinded window.
I listened to hymns and asked so much of them they quieted
like a body that withers when it feels itself
clung to. I was taught the body is deceptive.
The heart, deceptive.

Get out of me but stay with me, the city cried.
I had been looking up at the awnings with names,
trying to find a place for us. I am uncertain now,
but there was no moon. Shop lights on and off then off
for good. When Thomas asked to see the extent
of the wounded body, evidence
was consecrated as a holy request.
Evidence being that which screams its moment—
one need not even look.

KOI

After all the days and nights we've spent
with *Starry Messenger*, with Dante,
with Plato, his temperance
painted as a woman who pours
water into a bowl but does not spill.

After particle theory and the geologic time of this quartz
gilded beneath the roaming gone,
composites of limestone calculated down to the animal
that laid upon it and quietly died.

After hearing how camels carted away the broken
Colossus of Rhodes, showing us how to carry
and build back our destroyed selves,

hearing there was once a hand
that first learned to turn
an infant right in the womb,

that there was, inside Michelangelo, an Isaiah to carve out
the David, *the idea*, the one buried
in us who can slay the enormities.

After all visions and prophecies that made the heart large,
once and again, true or untrue,

after learning to shave the gleaming steel down—
the weapon, the bomb we make,
and the watercolor made after
of the dropped-upon crowd, thin strokes
over a pale wash—
                          after all this, still

one of us can't know another. Once, under
an iron sky, I listened
to a small assemblage of voices.
Two by two broke off into the field
to strip down the unbroken flock of starling dark
between them. The ceremony of the closing in,
the hope each to each might not stay tourists
before the separate, chiseled ruin of the other:

the unspeakable, the illegible one before us—

this is what the linguists call the dead, isn't it?

But how are you, we say,
meaning how have you been made,
what is wrong, what
happened, we ask, how long have you been waiting,
are you on my side, can you promise to stay,
will you keep
the etchings clear on my stone
and come visit me, your never-known,

                              will you lean over my ghost
how we leaned over the green pools of the Japanese garden,
a cluster of lanterns blowing out above us
wisp by wisp, a school of koi testing the surface,
letting us look all the way in
until we saw each eye
                    was like a net heaped on shore.

Just like our eyes, weren't they? All accidents, wastes,
all saving needs filled and unfilled, the cracked shells,
the kelp fronds torn from their buoys, all caught here,
inside us—
        the seven we loved, the six we lost—
seaglass, the living
and the human, alone.

III

Colosseum

It was as though I had lived a
little, wandered a little, until I
came to the precipice, and I
clearly saw that there was nothing
ahead except ruin.

LEO TOLSTOY

OVERTURE

It's grief that tears the paper lanterns
right where the calligraphy begins to tell
of the ferocious heart
of some other dynasty
that boasted persimmons and pomegranate,
what it grew and how it warred
while its people floated dead
on flooded rice fields.

My stoic, unconvinced world,
world of the paper heart,
is it that you don't know grief
or haven't had enough of it
that you let yourself
be governed so?

COLOSSEUM

I stared at the ruin, the powder of the dead
now beneath ground, a crowd
assembled and breathing with
indiscernible sadnesses, light
from other light, far off
and without explanation. Somewhere unseen
the ocean deepened then and now
into more ocean, the black fins
of the bony fish obscuring
its bottommost floor, carcasses of mollusks
settling, casting one last blur of sand,
unable to close again. Next to me a woman,
the seventeen pins it took to set
her limb, to keep every part flush with blood.

     ~

In the book on the ancient mayfly
which lives only four hundred minutes
and is, for this reason, called *ephemeral*,
I couldn't understand why the veins laid across
the transparent sheets of wings, impossibly
fragile, weren't blown through in their half-day
of flight. Or how that design has carried the species
through antiquity with collapsing
horses, hailstorms and diffracted confusions of light.

     ~

If I remember correctly what's missing
broke off all at once, not into streets
but into rows portioned off for shade as it
fell here, the sun there
where the poled awning ended. Didn't the heat

and dust funnel down
to the condemned as they fought
until the animal took them completely? Didn't at least one stand
perfectly still?

⁓

I said to myself: Beyond my husband there are strange trees
growing on one of the seven hills.
They look like intricately tended bonsais, but
enormous and with unreachable hollows.
He takes photographs for our black folios,
thin India paper separating one from another.
There is no scientific evidence of consciousness
lasting outside the body. I think when I die
it will be completely.

⁓

But it didn't break off all at once.
It turns out there is a fault line under Rome
that shook the theater walls
slight quake by quake. After the empire fell
the arena was left untended
and exotic plants spread a massive overgrowth,
their seeds carried from Asia and Africa, sown accidentally
in the waste of the beasts.
Like our emptying, then aching questions,
the vessel filled with unrecognizable faunas.

⁓

How great is the darkness in which we grope,
William James said, not speaking of the earth, but the mind
split into its caves and plinth from which to watch
its one great fight.

And then, when it is over,
when those who populate your life return
to their curtained rooms and lie down without you,
you are alone, you
are quarry.

~

When the mayflies emerge it is in great numbers
from lakes where they have lived in nymphal skins
through many molts. At the last
a downy skin is shed and what proofed them
is gone. Above water there is
nothing for them to feed on—

they don't even look, except for each other.

They form hurried swarms in that starving, sudden hour
and mate fully. When it is finished it is said
the expiring flies gather beneath boatlights
or lampposts and die under them minutely,
drifting down in a flock called *snowfall.*

~

Nothing wants to break, but this wanted to break,
built for slaughter, open arches to climb through,
lines of glassless squares above, elaborate
pulleys raising the animals on platforms
out of the passaged darkness.

When one is the site of so much pain, one must pray
to be abandoned.

SNAKES

It is difficult to be in the museum with you now,
the shining floors abiding beneath our feet.
And the display
of tools the earlier versions of ourselves
used to grind corn to meal.
Dear listener, you don't know how jealous
I have become of such images of simplicity,
however much they lie. I die a little.
In New Orleans, snakes followed the flood
into the houses. They moved
like completely sane machines, able to execute
their bodies perfectly. Little storms all over,
coil after coil of mimicry.
How wise for the living plagues
to leave only their effects for archaeologists
to find—here is a life
to unearth, although eaten
farther down than expected.
It's not the bowl of dust that lasts,
nor drought, cholera, or sting,
but the ax that cracked the attic
when there was no more breath.
All that will be found are homes and tools of stone.
Not what buried them into their unlit,
quick graves, but what saved them
a moment longer
will abide.

ROSE

Remember the great games of the arenas
how the officials would flood them then fill them

with eels and dolphins ships for battle

now I build a miniature menagerie
to study creatures under the enormous
pressure of all that's dead in them

just today Rose and I put her stone animals
upright again on the mantel

the granite wildebeest chipped thin by migration
so near her extinguished gazelle

she tries to face them
toward some center of the room
where perhaps her husband is—

she has to shift them all the time

DUOMO

There are animals of the savannah listening
through the ground, still hearing
with all of their bodies—shaking
when they feel another shaken as prey
or suddenly stilled in the unseen
fields scattered with paperbarks, lightly-silvered
shade, acacia now and then,
and sound.
        Miles the sound extends into all
the nettings, across fractured streets, through
apartment floors from which it feels
there is no coming down.
But we move unhearing, unheard, in cruel
ambiguity beneath the amber-letting trees
draping house to house,
weeping down the thought
of yellow morning—
        how yellow will come
over everything, over you and me
as we wake, over a Florence gone,
unreachable to us now—gone the bridge
that survived the war,
its diamond shops and paperies,
paisley waterspills curved over parchment
how oils seeped out of the ghost rigs
and left slow blankets over egrets and gulls feeding
on the blackened cargo of the surface.
        The aurora
was beautiful on those killing spirals, quiet
as maize-light on the apostles
settled in caverns of the great dome
built on the copper edge of the middle ages.

The dome draws our slightest vibrations into it now,
though miles and storms away,
holding the said, the wept, the unheard
in its arch of yellowwood vaults.
It's so watery here
where we are promised to be saved:
Here, in memory's latest light
where the iron doors of the baptistry close
to the tourists
and to the whispering dead
as our sounds fall delicately, fall
privately into the bottom
of the devastated font.

EASTER EVENING

In the haze of cold April,
when the birds draw their necks deep
into their bodies on the electric wire
like a string of dead lights, when last year's locust shells
are dried of their tissues and shift in the grasses of the riverbank,
rye and bluestem and reddened cordgrass, three floras braided,
then loosened, then snapping in the wind like a promise
given and taken back, it's at this moment,

parked by the river, that ice blooms shattered asters
across the windshield like eyes pried open,
the clear glass a starved sheet of mind
with something finally written on it
by that anonymous finger.

But then it's gone, and I know this is how it is for us:
We are told things but they melt away.
And when the words go, or when we know
instruction was never
there, a great absence comes like a sky
with all its living creatures huddled against the part of us
split open at the tip by weather
or desire, the garden we rake and rake again
until there's nothing left but the waiting.

This is what we ask the dead god to rise into.

But it isn't the right request, and he grows quieter
than the silence he already kept,
as when a man decides to leave a woman, decides this is
the only thing that can be done to save both.
In this way we are told it is over.

EARTH

Wild horses folded into their last night.
One burrowed against the dead's descending heat
as three cantered from the threadbare wood.

You must leave everything lit
by city light and Damascus light, anything fueled
except by your eyes on these animal bodies.

Species by species, light by light.

As for the tarpan it shall be for you.
A reckoning so slow you aren't even frightened.

DIVINING STICK

There is no promise from this earth,
though it speaks. Finches
fly from industrial firesmoke,
the low river lies
beside laborers who build back
the entire collapse.

It is June, month of the agate.
In the little watermarked house
I tie the stone to a broom
to make a divining stick. The agate
turns on a yellow thread and gives
a dull chime where metal keeps the straw tight.
I lift it up, I circle it above me.
Where will the water be? I whisper.
Where won't it be, it answers.

SEAWATER, AND OURS A
BED ABOVE IT

We wished that if we raked
the sea-carved skeletons from beneath
the house the true soft back of earth
would show a constant bone.
But those same shells trawled from the gulf
held back malarial waters
confused by houses raised above them.

We said this house is breaking
when one end sank and one beam cracked—
(in my honest sleep I said
our house is dead)—
as our hound clicked over the floors,
scratching the same raw second
we did not learn the law of,

that we live and die and live again
into dawns we feel it is right
to wash only our feet in the basin,
letting the water pass over us
into the ground.

And we do know, don't we:
We will be overcome by waters
where I stand with my lanterns and cans,
my useless preparations and provisions,
with the God I loved, I hated, and you.

I might not know you, nor you,
me, even though we've washed each other
with salt. But we know how we will end:

Waters will sweep the shells over our eyes,
and we will recognize
where we are
from what we saw
in museums and papers, from what we heard
in the agate voice of the scientist
who spoke in the quiet
only the truth need not rise above,

who, somewhere inland, takes tourists
through a glass garden
where tropicals and ferns
are rained on periodically
by a false mist
to show how spores used to shine
from even the underside of the world.

EARTH,
THIS FIRELIT LANTERN

will master the heart
only in its last hour
of wicking down, flickering to light
its own wounds and mishandlings,
what's been taken and what collected
on this extinguishing thing.

You whose love once left
but returned
must forget
your human analogy.

Deadly to believe a heaven
might include you.

You had a heaven.
You were its gods.

Notes

The epigraph for *Colosseum* is from *Trilogy* by H.D., part I, "The Walls Do Not Fall," which she wrote during the bombing of London during World War II.

The epigraph for "Storm" is from the ancient epic, *The Curse of Akkad*, written a century after the fall of the Akkadian Empire, roughly 2100 B.C. Elizabeth Kolbert's *Field Notes from a Catastrophe: Man, Nature, and Climate Change*, details how the Akkadian Empire collapsed due to a severe, 300-year drought. The ruins are believed to lie south of Baghdad.

The epigraph for "Tolstoy's Storm" is from *Confession* by Leo Tolstoy, translated by David Patterson (W. W. Norton).

The epigraph for "Vessel" is from *Selected Poems* by Marina Tsvetaeva, translated by Elaine Feinstein (Penguin Books).

"Tess" is dedicated to Tess Gallagher.

The epigraph for "Spring Wish" is from poem 1651, *The Poems of Emily Dickinson: Variorum Edition*. Ed. R. W. Franklin (The Belknap Press of Harvard University Press).

"Coliseum Theater" is at 1233 Coliseum Street in New Orleans. The theater burned on February 3, 2006, six months after the flood. Fires were common after Hurricane Katrina due to gas leaks, electrical start-ups, and arson. The *New Orleans Times-Picayune* reported, "A three-alarm fire Friday afternoon destroyed the historic Coliseum Theater, the 91-year-old gem in the lower Garden District that was a reminder of days when such neighborhood movie houses dotted the city."

"Koi": *Starry Messenger* was published by Galileo Galilei in 1610. "Temperance," one of the four platonic virtues, is depicted by Antonio Pollaiolo and hangs in the Uffizi Gallery of Florence, Italy. The Colossus of Rhodes, one of the Seven Wonders of the Ancient World, broke at the knees during an earthquake in 226 B.C., it is said, having spanned the harbor entrance for only 54 years. "The seven we loved, the six we lost" refers to a statistic I once heard that humans fall in love, on average, seven times during their lives.

The epigraph for "Colosseum" is from Tolstoy's *Confession*.

"Colosseum" quotes William James from the end of his book, *Psychology: The Briefer Course*. Ed. Gordon Allport (Harper Torchbooks, 1961).

"Rose" is dedicated to Rose Preston.

"Earth [Wild horses folded . . .]": "In 1879, pursued by humans, the last wild, pure tarpan mare fell down a crevasse in Ukraine and died; the last captive died eight years later in a Moscow zoo" (*Smithsonian* magazine, November 2007).

Katie Ford is the author of *Deposition* and a chapbook, *Storm*. Her poems have appeared in *American Poetry Review*, the *New Yorker*, the *Paris Review*, *Ploughshares*, *Poets & Writers*, and *Seneca Review*. She has received awards and grants from the Academy of American Poets and the PEN American Center, and she received a 2008 Lannan Literary Fellowship. Ford teaches at Franklin and Marshall College and lives in Philadelphia with her husband, the novelist Josh Emmons.

The text of *Colosseum* has been set in Cochin, designed by Georges Peignot and named after the French engraver Charles Nicolas Cochin. Composition by BookMobile Design and Publishing Services. Manu factured by Versa Press on acid-free paper.